How My Bike was Made

Fiona Macdonald

OXFORD

UNIVERSITY PRESS

OXFORD
UNIVERSITY PRESS

Great Clarendon Street, Oxford, OX2 6DP

Oxford University Press is a department of the University of Oxford.
It furthers the University's objective of excellence in research, scholarship,
and education by publishing worldwide in

Oxford New York

Athens Auckland Bangkok Bogotá Buenos Aires Calcutta
Cape Town Chennai Dar es Salaam Delhi Florence Hong Kong Istanbul
Karachi Kuala Lumpur Madrid Melbourne Mexico City Mumbai
Nairobi Paris São Paulo Singapore Taipei Tokyo Toronto Warsaw
and associated companies in Berlin Ibadan

Oxford is a registered trade mark of Oxford University Press
in the UK and in certain other countries

A CIP record for this book is available from the British Library

ISBN 0 19 915589 5
Available in packs
Toys Pack of Six   (one of each book)   ISBN 0 19 915595 X
Toys Class Pack   (six of each book)   ISBN 0 19 915617 4

Printed in Hong Kong

Acknowledgements

The publisher would like to thank Corbis UK for permission to
reproduce the photograph on page 3.

Location photography Martin Sookias, studio photograhy Mark Mason.
Front cover photograph Stephen Oliver.

With special thanks to the management and staff of Dawes Cycles,
Birmingham, for their technical advice, and assistance with the location
photography, and the Hinksey Heights Golf Course, Oxford.

Contents

Mountain bikes

This is my mountain bike. I ride it on roads and grass. This book will tell you how it was made.

The first mountain bikes were made for adults.
They were made in the United States of America.

Designing the bike

The bike was designed to be safe and comfortable to ride. It has many special features.

a cushioned saddle to make it comfortable

big tyres to stop it skidding

gears to make it easy to ride up hills

a strong frame

good brakes to help it stop quickly

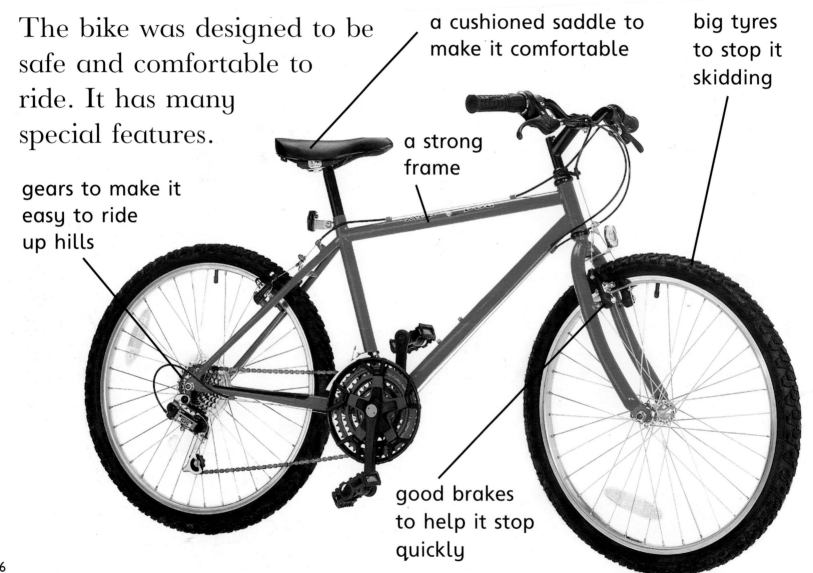

The bike was designed by engineers.

They drew plans for the bike on a computer.

They tested the metal on special machines.

The materials

The bike was made from different materials.

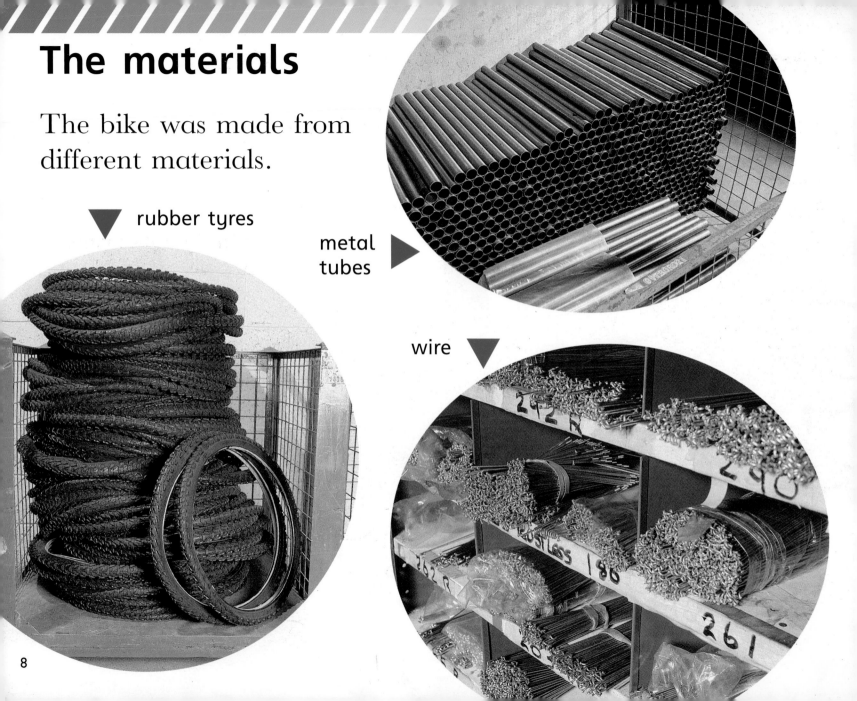

rubber tyres

metal tubes

wire

Making the frame

First, the frame was made out of metal tubes.

The tube was cut
into sections. ▼

The tubes were
put together. ▼

Then the tubes were
stuck together. This is
called "brazing". ▼

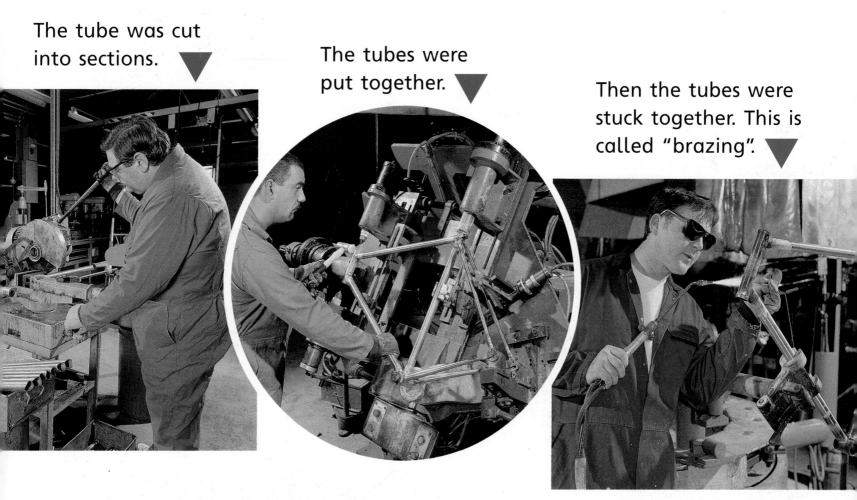

Painting the frame

Next, the frame was painted.

It was painted with grey "primer" paint. ▼

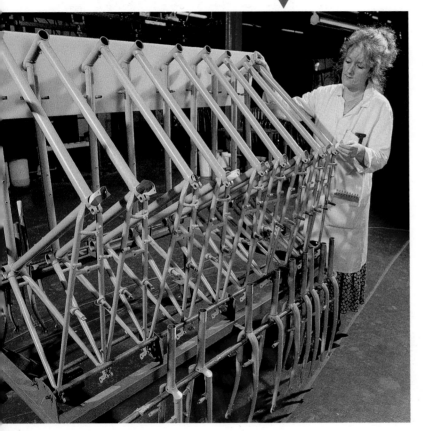

The red paint was put on next.

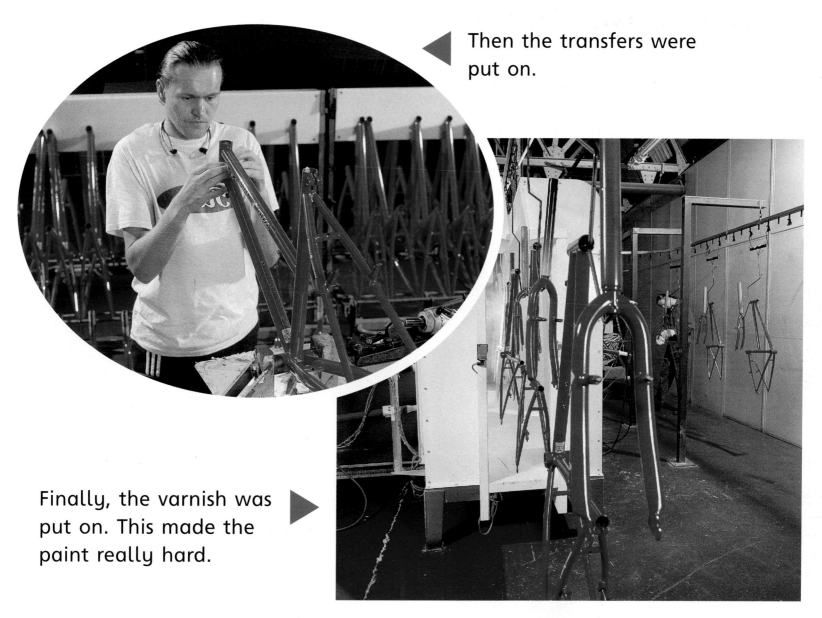

Then the transfers were put on.

Finally, the varnish was put on. This made the paint really hard.

Wheels

The wheels were made next.

The spokes were put into the wheels.

spokes

The tyres were put on.

12

Brakes, gears, and handlebars

The brake levers were put on to the handlebars.

The gear wheels were put on to the frame.

The handlebars were put on to the frame.

Putting the bike together

Finally, the parts of the bike were put together.

chain

wheels

saddle

The bike was wrapped in cardboard to protect it.

I bought the bike!

Index